The Miami: The History and Legacy of the Native American Tribe across the Great Lakes and Oklahoma

By Charles River Editors

George Catlin's painting of Miami Chief *Kee-món-saw*

About Charles River Editors

Charles River Editors provides superior editing and original writing services across the digital publishing industry, with the expertise to create digital content for publishers across a vast range of subject matter. In addition to providing original digital content for third party publishers, we also republish civilization's greatest literary works, bringing them to new generations of readers via ebooks.

Sign up here to receive updates about free books as we publish them, and visit Our Kindle Author Page to browse today's free promotions and our most recently published Kindle titles.

Introduction

Seneca Chief Cornplanter

When the American Revolution ended, the United States and Britain reached an impressively comprehensive peace in the Treaty of Paris. Among the important terms of the treaty, Britain recognized the colonies as free and relinquished territorial claims to them. The two sides then negotiated the boundaries that separated the United States from the British colonies in present-day Canada. Additionally, the British and Americans strove to share certain waters, including the Mississippi River and the fishing waters off Newfoundland. Finally, the two sides made mutual promises regarding paying debts and returning property that had been confiscated during the war, including slaves.

Still, the Treaty of Paris was not without its problems. Almost immediately, individual states in America rejected certain provisions and ignored them outright, a hallmark characteristic of American federalism that would lead to the Civil War 80 years later. Other problems included disputes along the boundary with Canada, and the fact that American access to the Mississippi River was blocked after the British and Spanish signed a separate treaty that left Spain in control of Florida. Some of these problems would fester heading into the 19th century, and eventually the British and Americans would go to war again in 1812.

The new United States was faced with a fundamental problem: to expand, it had to settle lands to the west of the Appalachian Mountains, ceded to it by the British. However, the mountains were occupied by Native American groups who had no desire to make way for white settlers. The treaty had created a vast frontier for the fledgling nation, and any American settlers pushing west along it were bound to encounter hostile natives.

For the most part, the conflicts that followed consisted mostly of the Native Americans suffering defeat in the face of a better-equipped adversary, interspersed with binding treaties, which, on the side of the federal government, proved not very binding at all. Occasionally, however, there arose a Native American leader of such ability that such defeats were temporarily reversed, and Little Turtle, the war chief of the Miami tribe, was one such man. Under his leadership, a confederation of Miami and other tribes inflicted the worst defeat ever suffered by an American army in the newly independent nation. Almost a quarter of the Army's total strength was lost in a single battle, but while later Native American leaders such as Sitting Bull and Crazy Horse have become legends, Little Turtle is not as well-remembered. This is particularly odd, given that he actually defeated the American military and helped shape the development of the nascent United States and its military.

The short war between a confederation of Native American tribes under Little Turtle's leadership has been referred to by many names, including the Northwest Indian War, the Ohio War, and the Miami War, but it is probably best known as Little Turtle's War. Before Little Turtle's War, it was believed that the U.S. did not need a professional army; that ordinary citizens would take up arms in times of threat and serve in militias as they had done in the fight against the British. After this war, the U.S. government was forced to recognize the need for a professional standing army. The country was thus fundamentally changed by Little Turtle's War, the cause of which was mainly due to the military brilliance of a single Miami warrior.

As for Little Turtle's people, the Miami originally called themselves Twightwee, after the cry of the crane, their symbol. Like the majestic crane, they are a quiet, but powerful people. "Miami" is actually derived from the name that the tribe was called by the Ojibwe Indians, Myaamia, which means "the downstream people," reflecting their home among the lakes and rivers of the American Midwest. This moniker was altered by French settlers into "Miami," that we know today. Rich tribal history is passed down from generation to generation. After millennia living and thriving in the wilderness with other native groups, life would change drastically for the Miami in a mere three centuries after the New World was colonized by Europeans. They were almost eliminated completely by war and disease. European explorers reported the tribe to have at least fifteen thousand members in the early 1600s, but only about three thousand remained by 1736. British estimates after 1763 found about two thousand remaining. An 1825 estimate by Americans counted the Miami population at around 1,600. By the late 1800s, less than eight hundred remained. Through intertribal warfare, conflict with three different national governments, and complete loss of their homeland and way of life, the Miami people have maintained their culture while adapting to the changing world around them.

The Miami: The History and Legacy of the Native American Tribe across the Great Lakes and Oklahoma examines the movement of the Miami from their origins to their displacement in the 19th century. Along with pictures of important people, places, and events, you will learn about the Miami like never before.

The Miami: The History and Legacy of the Native American Tribe across the Great Lakes and Oklahoma

The Miami's Culture

The Miami tribe originally belonged to the huge Algonquin group of northeast North America which dates back to 1000 CE, according to Dr. Karen Carr from Cornell University. They probably traveled to North America from Siberia via a land bridge and mainly spoke the Algonquin language. Among other tribes, according to historian Lee Sultzman, the Miami had the reputation of being slow-spoken and polite.

Miami culture centered around two things, religion and food acquisition, both of which were strongly tied to the natural world they lived in. The Miami worshipped the sun and thunder, but they did not honor a plethora of deities as some other native tribes did. Totems, emblems believed to have spiritual significance, were important in Miami culture. They adopted several animal totems, including the wolf, loon, eagle, buzzard, panther, turkey, raccoon, elk, turtle, and crane, and they also honored totems of snow, sun, and water. Storytelling was also very important to the Miami culture. Without a written language, they relied on oral tradition to pass their culture on to new generations. The Great Spirit, their principal god, is believed to have created the world. They also honor a hero called Wisakatchekwa, and fear Thunder-Beings, mischievous forest sprites called Payiihsa, Maneto, a horned serpent that eats people, and True Tiger, an underwater monster who causes people to drown.

The hallmark of Miami religion was the Midewiwin, or Grand Medicine Society, a revered religious organization whose leaders were believed able to heal the sick, bring the death of enemies, secure a successful hunt or harvest, and gain supernatural assistance in battle. Sacred medicinal, magical objects were important in many Miami rites and ceremonies. The Midewiwin consisted of hundreds of members, including shamans, prophets, seers, and chiefs who passed a complex series of initiation rites in a special medicine lodge, centering on the symbolic death and rebirth of the initiate.

The Miami had principal settlements along the Wabash, Blue, Eel, Scioto, and Ohio Rivers. They occupied some of the most lush and picturesque lands in the American Midwest, sandy plateaus covered in shrub oak and evergreen trees, crystal springs, rivers, and lakes. They went on to build communities throughout the wetlands, prairies, woodlands, and river bottoms of present-day Indiana which maintained a common language and common hunting, farming, and cultural practices. Their ancient home, the Great Lakes region, contains hundreds of lakes of all sizes, which teem with waterfowl, bass, pickerel and other fish, and serve as watering holes for red deer, muskrat, wild turkeys, prairie chicken, pheasants, otter, beaver, and all species of animals which they hunted for skins and food.

Living near rivers and lakes, water was a huge part of the Miami's life. They made dugout canoes by hollowing out large trees. Over land, they used dogs as pack animals which carried gear on their backs and pulled wooden sleds called travois.

For generations, the seasons dominated the lives of the Miami people. During spring and summer, the Miami resided in permanent agricultural villages that consisted of rectangular longhouses, wood-framed structures with high gabled roofs about twelve by twenty feet in size and covered with elm bark. A separate, larger building was used for councils and ceremonies, and there were usually sweat lodges. According to Stewart Rafert's book, *The Miami Indians of Indiana,* the Miami people spent most of their time outdoors; homes were mainly for sleeping and storage, as well as shelter from bad weather. Most working, cooking, and eating was done outside.

The Miami women grew white corn and other vegetables in the fertile soil of the river valleys, processing and drying their crops to last throughout the year. According to Sultzman, their corn was generally regarded as superior to that of other tribes because it had a fine skin and could be ground into a smoother meal. Corn was usually stored in bark-lined underground pits about eight feet in diameter and up to six feet deep so that it could be used year-round. Miami leadership usually chose high ridges overlooking the placid lakes as village sites. Fertile soil was productive for crops of corn, squash, melons, and gourds, and many food species grew wild: strawberries, grapes, plums, hazelnuts, acorns, and medicinal plants. They used natural clay for pottery and reeds in the marshes for matting.

After the harvest as the weather began to cool, the entire village moved to nearby prairies for a communal buffalo hunt, then separated into smaller winter hunting camps to the east and west of the River Valley, where the men hunted white tail deer, elk, and a wide variety of smaller animals and birds through the winter. Upon arrival at the hunting camp, women set to work building *wikiami*, dome-shaped lodges made of saplings covered with mats or bark with a fire pit in the center, storage at the rear, and sleeping platforms along the sides, that could be completed in a couple of hours.

One of their main hunting methods was using controlled burns to drive animals toward the hunters who stood ready with bows and arrows, tomahawks, and spears. According to Rafert, they sometimes killed as many as two hundred bison a day. The slain animals were divided equally according to the number of people in a family. The meat that was not eaten immediately was sun dried or broiled on gridirons, allowing it to last for months.

In the early spring, the women and children moved to the sugar maple groves to collect sap which they made into maple syrup for eating and trading. When the weather began to get warmer again, they returned to their villages, and the women began clearing fields and planting crops, and the agricultural cycle began again.

There were six major bands that made up the Miami Confederacy: Atchakangouen, Kilatika, Mengkonkia, Pepikokia, Piankashaw, and Wea. They were each independent of the others with their own chief, but they spoke the same language and had similar cultural practices.

The Miami Nation was a society of strongly interconnected communities because they mandated exogamous clans, meaning that members were required to marry outside their clan, or extended family. In Miami culture, polygamy was common. Iconic Chief Little Turtle had two wives who lived under the same roof in harmony, according to Calvin Young's book, *Little Turtle: the Great Chief of the Miami Indian Nation.*

Young describes the average Miami as being of medium build, agreeable, and athletic, and it was common for both men and women to have tattoos all over the body. Men wore little clothing except in winter, but women usually wore deerskin dresses with leggings. Both men and women wore leather moccasins, but did not don elaborate headdresses, preferring beaded headbands with a few red feathers. Miami men usually shaved their heads and wore a porcupine roach, a small headdress made of the spiky hair of the porcupine. Women grew their hair long and wore it braided or in buns. Chiefs were known for dressing more flamboyantly.

The Miami might have been extremely hard workers, but they enjoyed a game or two during their free time. They played several sporting games, including shooting arrows at balls thrown in the air, a version of stacking cups, a type of bowling, and sliding wooden planks on ice in the winter. These games usually involved friendly wagers, and villages competed against each other. Miami youth also competed in swimming, shooting, wrestling, and lacrosse.

Miami tribal government consisted of a council of village chiefs led by an elected head chief. Each village had a civil chief who usually inherited the office from his father, a war chief who was chosen based on his talent for leading raids, and female chiefs, the oldest daughters of both civil and war chiefs. Civil chiefs were responsible for regulation of the village and negotiations for peace, while war chiefs planned battle strategy, sent out military parties, and led war rituals, and female chiefs supervised major feasts, reported affairs of the village to the male chiefs, and helped prepare war parties. There was also a *kapia,* or steward to the civil chief, who distributed goods and carried messages for the chief. In Miami culture, chiefs were given the utmost respect and ceremony. A unanimous vote by the tribal council is still required to override a chief's decisions. Groups from different villages often came together to negotiate peace with neighboring tribes and European settlers in tribal council meetings.

Warfare

Although largely a peaceful people, the Miami's history was shaped by conflict, first with other Native American tribes and then with European nations. The Miami tribe numbered about 15,000 at the beginning of the seventeenth century. Although large and powerful, the Miami Confederacy was not as dominant as their enemies, the Iroquois League, which consisted of six tribes: the Mohawks, Oneidas, Onondagas, Cayugas, Senecas, and Tuscaroras. They controlled areas from the plains of the Mississippi River to the Atlantic Ocean, and from the Tennessee River to the St. Lawrence River. The Miami formed a confederacy in opposition to the powerful Iroquois who were known as bloodthirsty conquerors. The fierce Lakota tribes to the west and the Iroquois in the east had squeezed several tribes, including the Miami, Illinois, Potawatomi, and Mascouten, between Lake Michigan and the Mississippi, so these tribes fought over land there and moved around often.

Around 1640, a fierce and cruel territorial war began to rage between the Miami and Iroquois that forced many tribes in the area to abandon their homelands. Tribal clashes among the Miami, Winnebago, Fox, Wea, and others forced the Miami to relocate farther inland on the Fox River in 1660; with some groups even moving to the Mississippi River near the current Illinois-Wisconsin border. Thousands of warriors from both sides were slain during years of conflict.

War was not entered into lightly by the Miami. A sacred and methodical process took place before any military activity was undertaken, as described by Rafert. Before declaring war on anyone or planning any military endeavors, various war chiefs met in council for discussion and strategy-making. Once a decision to go to war was made, a meeting of warriors took place at the council house, where plans were discussed and explained. Younger warriors prepared for the war party by cooking food, chopping wood, preparing equipment and clothing, and packing. The night before departure, the tribe shaman led an all-night war ceremony. Sometimes, women who felt the need to join the war party were allowed to do so. One such woman successfully led a retaliatory war party against the Iroquois, but unfortunately, her name was never recorded.

As European settlers encroached on native lands, the hunting grounds of the Miami were even more limited. Invasions by the Iroquois further exacerbated the situation, and wars between the confederacies became frequent. Armed with guns obtained from the Dutch in New York, Iroquois war parties continually raided and terrorized their neighboring tribes. The Miami could not successfully withstand the continuous assaults, and they fled west, forming a confederacy with their new neighbors.

In the 1670s, the Miami migrated south and east toward their old territory as threats from the Iroquois decreased, and by 1681, there were several thousand Miami on the St. Joseph River.

As much as the Miami disliked the Iroquois, they hated the Illinois even more. When the Iroquois went to war with the Illinois over beaver hunting grounds in 1680, the Miami allied with the Iroquois and Seneca to drive most of the Illinois west of the Mississippi, allowing the Miami to retake their land east of the great river. A war with the Dakota Sioux in 1692, however, resulted in the loss of territories on the Chicago River and part of the Mississippi Valley. The alliance with the Iroquois went south when the Miami allowed groups of their enemies, the Shawnee, to settle among them. French explorers arranged a peace treaty between the Miami and Illinois in 1682, and the Miami Confederacy began to concentrate near Fort St. Louis, a French trading post on the Illinois River. Two years later, the Seneca, a branch of the Iroquois, returned to attack Miami villages in Indiana and then swept west, but were halted at Fort St. Louis.

In 1687, while Miami warriors were absent hunting, the Seneca, who were known to cannibalize those they conquered, destroyed their village near Chicago, taking several women and children prisoner. Miami warriors eventually caught up with the Seneca and killed most of them.

That same year, the French encouraged the Miami and other tribes to unite against the Iroquois. The French gave assistance to the Miami Confederacy against the Iroquois, as it was in their interest to have peace among the natives which led to easier and more profitable fur trade. A great and decisive battle took place on the banks of Maumee, in which the French and Miami defeated the Iroquois. This led to a lasting peace. Continued raids forced the Iroquois to retreat across the Great Lakes to New York by 1690.

By 1700, the Miami had returned to their homelands in present day Indiana and formed new settlements at the south end of Lake Michigan, on the Kalamazoo River, and on the St. Joseph River. Their population, however, had been cut in half by war and disease. French authorities arranged a conference of all warring tribes in Montreal in 1701, and a peace treaty was created, ending fifty years of civil war between the Iroquois and the Great Lakes tribes.

The same year, French governor Antoine Cadillac built Fort Pontchartrain at Detroit for trade with the Great Lakes tribes. He invited nearly every tribe in the area to settle at his new post, including the Miami, and the overcrowding and competition for the region's limited resources exacerbated rivalries which further weakened the alliance between the Algonquins and Iroquois. An outbreak of smallpox in 1704 further worsened conditions.

Under less pressure from the Iroquois, the Miami and other Great Lakes tribes were able to expand into territory south and east, nearer to the Wabash River. Exploring down the Great Lakes and then along the rivers running off of them, Miami leaders found an ideal spot at the junction of the St. Mary's and St. Joseph Rivers at the head of the Maumee River near present-day Fort Wayne, Indiana. Here, they established their principal village, called Kekionga. Placement at the head of a river and the convergence of trails leading to Lake Michigan and Detroit made Kekionga an economic and political center for the tribe. Levying tolls at the Wabash-Maumee portage gave the Miami a significant economic boost. Early French explorers described the village as being surrounded by gardens, orchards, and extensive cornfields. Since Kekionga was located on the boundary between French and English territory, the Miami maintained a large degree of independence from both nations.

Dealing with the French

A map of major Native American tribes in the Northwest Territory

Unique cultures have been developing in North America for more than 10,000 years, and given the separation between the Native American peoples and other developing civilizations across the oceans, this led to the emergence of a very distinct and different way of life. However, things changed when the first settlers from Europe began to arrive in the Americas near the end of the 15th century.

Unlike South and Central America, which were both initially settled by the Spanish, the first Europeans in North America were French fishermen who arrived in the area looking for cod in the Grand Banks off the coast of Newfoundland. They built small settlements ashore where they could rest, repair their ships, and preserve their catches for transporting back to Europe. They also met the Native American people and quickly realized they were willing to trade furs for metal items, such as knives.

At that time, fur was a valuable and desired commodity in Europe, mostly used for making warm and high-status clothing. Before the Age of Exploration, most fur in Europe came from Scandinavia and Russia and was relatively expensive, but now, a new source of fur was discovered, and pelts were available in exchange for mere trinkets. The French fishermen soon realized they could make more money by trading for furs than bringing their catches to market, leading to the development of the first trading posts in Newfoundland and near present-day Quebec.

Initially, these weren't supported or sponsored by the French government - they were commercial operations set up by canny merchants. Naturally, it did not take long for merchants from other countries to recognize the trade potential in the New World, and the French were soon joined by British and Dutch settlements on the East Coast. As these merchants came into conflict, different Native American allies joined the various sides. The French merchants dealt with a confederacy of mainly Algonquian-speaking Native American tribes in the Great Lakes region, in addition to the warlike Huron people. British and Dutch traders mainly dealt with an Iroquois confederation led by the Mohawk people, who also happened to be longstanding, traditional enemies of the Huron. This ensured that when competition turned to conflict, the Native Americans would also be drawn in.

The first of what became known as the Indian Wars erupted over the fur trade. During the Beaver Wars, the British and Dutch supplied their allies, the Mohawk, with firearms and other weapons, and the French soon followed suit to arm the Huron. Settlers would exploit traditional enmities between the natives for their own ends, and not for the last time. The supply of modern weapons, however, meant that these conflicts were more destructive than any that had come before. For example, in 1628, the Mohawk attacked and virtually wiped out the Mahican people, an event commemorated in an 1826 novel by James Fenimore Cooper, *The Last of the Mohicans*.

The Beaver Wars continued until the signing of the Great Peace of Montreal in 1701 between Britain and France (by that time, the Dutch had been driven out of their colonies in North America). Despite the treaty, sporadic violence would continue between British and French settlers, often supported by allied Native American tribes, until the signature of the Treaty of Paris in 1763, through which Britain gained control of many French colonies in North America.

There is no question that the introduction of firearms and the use of Native American warriors to fight for colonial powers had a corrosive and destructive effect on Native American culture in present-day Canada and along the East Coast, but the settlers' introduction of firearms was not the main cause. In fact, the natives suffered far more as a result of foreign diseases and alcohol.

Most Europeans in the 17th and 18th centuries were reluctant to drink water and regarded beer, ale, and wine as safer and healthier alternatives. This made sense in Europe, particularly in towns and cities where sanitation was at best primitive, because most water supplies were contaminated. The water in the relatively unspoiled towns of North America was perfectly safe to drink, but settlers continued to prefer alcohol. They made wines from fruit and vegetables, cider from apples, and often ensured that the first large building completed in new settlements was a brewery.

By the mid-1700s, virtually every colonial British town had not just a brewery, but also a distillery to make rum from molasses and cane sugar imported from the Caribbean. Soon, astute traders realized they could trade alcohol, which was cheap to produce, to Native Americans for valuable furs and other items.

Most Native Americans had previously had no contact with alcohol. Some tribes did make wines and beers, but these had a relatively low alcohol content, and they were generally consumed during religious ceremonies, not for recreation. Thus, the sudden introduction of alcohol was a disaster for some tribes. Social structures, which had remained unchanged for thousands of years, disintegrated, and many Native Americans became addicted to the alcohol provided by settlers.

Though the introduction of alcohol had an immediate and harmful effect on many tribes coming into contact with settlers, there was another import that had a more direct effect. Many settlers brought diseases such as cholera and smallpox, which were previously unknown in North America and to which Native Americans had no natural immunity. The effects were devastating in every sense of the word. While the diseases brought by the settlers affected every Native American community with whom they had contact, in some cases, diseases virtually wiped out entire tribes. For example, in an area close to the British settlement at Massachusetts Bay, smallpox spread from the colonists to local tribes. By 1628, it is estimated that this disease had killed at least 90% of the Native American population in the surrounding area, including the populations of whole villages.

These diseases were not only transmitted through contact between settlers and Native Americans. Native American traders operated far inland and had contact with tribes who had never directly encountered white men. These traders unwittingly spread diseases, and soon, the Native American population across the continent was being decimated by disease.

Cynically, and most notoriously, some settlers used disease as a form of primitive biological weapon. After all, if a tribe was affected by disease, it would be easier for settlers to take their land, and there were a number of instances where items such as smallpox-infected blankets were given to Native Americans in a deliberate attempt to spread diseases. By then, the white settlers were largely immune, but they were quite fatal to the indigenous population.

Even before the Miami had contact with Europeans, the Europeans' presence was felt in a smallpox epidemic that swept north from Spanish explorers in Chile in the early sixteenth century. Although the Miami had no written records before Europeans arrived, it is likely that about 30% of the population died, and the disruption in food production and secondary pneumonia and streptococcal infections might have killed many more. In 1633-34, measles swept through the Great Lakes area from Europeans in eastern Canada, leading to hundreds of deaths.

This misfortune would continue for the next century. In 1715, a measles epidemic led to the death of about 1,400 Miami, leaving only 400 warriors. A 1733 smallpox outbreak killed 150.

The first European contact with the Miami came in the mid-1650s when French explorers Pierre-Esprit Radisson and Médard Chouart encountered them on the Fox River in Wisconsin. French Jesuit priest Gabriel Druillettes was the first to make a written record of the Miami nation in 1658, placing them near present-day Green Bay, Wisconsin. In 1665, French explorers and traders Nicolas Perrot and Toussaint Baudry visited a Miami village and were received warmly with a peace pipe ceremony, feast, and dancing. They recorded a village with about 5,000 warriors led by Chief Tetinchoua, and a total population around 20,000, the largest native village seen in the area. French explorer Nicholas Perrot first came into contact with them in 1668 when he visited their fortified village at the head waters of the Fox River. Two years later, he returned, and Jesuit priest Father Claude-Jean Allouez also made contact that year. They were found to be a powerful nation with an army of five thousand warriors. The Miami maintained close trading relationships with the French at Green Bay and provided guides who led Father Jacques Marquette and Louis Joliet to the Mississippi River in 1673. According to Young, Marquette described them as friendly, docile, and eager to listen. Christian missionaries often visited these villages briefly, but no successful missions were founded in the territory of the Miami.

In 1667, a peace treaty was reached between the Iroquois and French explorers which extended to the tribes of the western Great Lakes. This provided much-needed relief to the native tribes and allowed the French to resume their fur trade in the west unmolested. By the 1670s, French settlers and traders were numerous but unregulated. French-made goods quickly replaced or supplemented stone tools, clay pottery and other handmade items used by the Miami, according to Rafert. They traded beaver pelts and corn for these, as well as other items, such as knives, kettles, mirrors, brandy, tobacco, cloth, and, of course, guns. The Miami, whose villages were located on major rivers, controlled portage to their advantage, and the French administration regulated trade and provided some military protection in return. French traders often lived in Miami villages.

In 1679, French explorer René-Robert Cavelier, Sieur de La Salle arrived in Miami country with a company of 30 French soldiers, lieutenants and assistants and two Indian guides. La Salle and his men pulled their canoes to the bank of the Maumee River, alighted, and approached the natives bearing the pipe of peace. Seeing that the white men were on a friendly mission, Miami Chief Big Horn and three of his warriors met La Salle and his company. Through an interpreter,

La Salle told the Miami that they had come to establish a fur trading relationship with the tribes, offering them guns, powder, knives, hatchets, kettles, beads, and many other articles made in France in exchange for furs. Big Horn agreed, since the land was rich in fur animals. La Salle received permission to erect a trading post in one of the Miami villages and gifted the natives plentifully with tools, cloth, and more. That evening, a large feast was held in honor of the French visitors, with buffalo, bear, and deer meat, fish, fruit, cornbread, and honey. According to Young, La Salle called them "neat in dress, splendid of bearing, haughty of manners," and he further said they were the most civilized of all the Indian nations he had encountered.

This period is known as a relatively peaceful one for both the French and Indians. As long as neither side tried to dominate the other, a symbiotic political, economic, and social system remained workable for all, while each side retained its cultural anonymity. In fact, by the beginning of the 18th century, the French and Miami people were quite intermingled. French trading posts were often built within or very near to Miami villages. A trading post was established near Kekionga in 1719, and French Captain Vincennes built Fort Miami on the southern bank of the Maumee River in 1734. Many French traders and settlers incorporated themselves into Miami society and interracial marriage was common.

Because of this harmonious relationship with the French, a generation of mixed-race, or Métis, grew in numbers, and they had more marriages and offspring. This created a large number of Miami tribespeople of French descent who were subsequently quite comfortable dealing with European and American officials and businessmen. They often did not differentiate themselves as a separate social class, though they might be more acculturated and have more wealth and higher social standing with white officials than full-blooded natives. They often acted as intermediaries between the tribal leadership and white officials.

Nevertheless, from the beginning of European settlement in North America, native tribes were often treated as pawns in the competition for land, resources, and power between France and Britain. The rivalry between the nations, which had gone on for centuries, bled over to the new continent like a festering wound. French Catholic and British Protestant missionaries competed for Indians' souls, governments competed for resources and territory, traders competed for markets, and both nations lured native tribes to their side as military allies, not to help the natives secure their homelands or improve their lives, as they often advertised.

By the beginning of the 18th century, the Native Americans had learned to use this rivalry to their advantage. French traders depended on commerce with the Miami, but they were able to secure better prices by comparison shopping with the British. By the 1720s, the industrial revolution in Britain had begun producing better quality goods for cheaper prices, and the Miami increased trade with the British, while maintaining a French military alliance. The European nations used their native alliances to their own advantage as well, by motivating their allies to attack tribes who were allied to the other side. For example, the Miami raided the Chickasaw, who were British allies, in 1734.

In the 1730s, British westward expansion had increased. Traders from Pennsylvania were entering eastern Ohio, and land speculators organized the Ohio Company of Virginia, which received a grant of 500,000 acres on the upper Ohio River, encroaching on native lands there.

In King George's War, fought from 1744-1748, the Miami stood beside the French, but a British blockade of Canada cut off the supply of French trade goods, and most of the Miami were forced to switch sides to maintain supplies. In 1748, Miami Chief Memeskia signed a treaty at Lancaster, Pennsylvania allowing the British to build trading posts in Ohio. The French were in danger of losing not only Ohio, but the entire Great Lakes region, so they attempted to maintain their monopoly by force, punishing tribes who traded too much with the other side. They called on their allies, the Ottawa, to attack Memeskia's village, destroying it and killing the chief. The following July, the Miami, Potawatomi, and Sauk rejoined the French alliance.

In the early 1750s, the French began building a line of new forts across western Pennsylvania to isolate Ohio from British traders. Unfortunately, this area was also claimed by British settlers, and Virginia militia major George Washington and his troops arrived in 1754 with a demand to halt construction, which led to the French and Indian War, a major war fought from 1754-1763.

The Miami allied with the French during this war, but they were not very involved in the fighting. They joined some attacks on English settlements and defeated Braddock's British Army in the Battle of the Monongahela in July 1755. They attempted to sign a peace treaty with British trader George Croghan in 1757, but it was rejected by the Virginia legislature. French soldiers returned from Fort William Henry in New York carrying smallpox that same year, leading to another epidemic that swept through the Great Lakes region, taking its toll on the Miami. With the fall of Quebec in 1759, the French defeat was certain and British troops took control of most of the French forts in Indiana the next year. In 1760, the Miami Chief Aquenochquah signed a treaty with British troops under General Washington that settled trade practices and routes. For the Miami and other native tribes, this meant the end of their advantage in trade negotiations between the two European countries, as the British now held a monopoly on trade and ended annual gifts to chiefs, increased prices and restricted the supply of goods.

Ultimately, the Treaty of Paris of 1763 awarded all French territory east of the Mississippi to Britain and west of the Mississippi to Spain. The era of peaceful coexistence with the French ended, and the British had quite a different idea of their role in North America.

The British

The end of the conflict between France and Britain brought a brief period of peace to the Great Lakes area, but it wouldn't be long before the Miami were drawn into another international conflict. The Seven Years' War was a crushing defeat for the French and a resounding success for Great Britain, but the war itself put the British Empire deep in debt, and to help alleviate the burden, Parliament soon began to pass a number of additional taxes to repay the nation's war debts.

Many of the new taxes targeted the 13 American colonies, and the logic for raising revenue in the colonies was clear. After all, the Seven Years' War had begun in North America, and a great deal of Britain's war expenses had gone toward supporting and defending the colonies. Moreover, the colonies were relatively untaxed by Great Britain compared to England, Scotland, and Wales, and no member of Parliament represented the 13 colonies, so Parliament could increase taxes on the colonies without a great deal of Parliamentary opposition or backlash among British citizens.

This last fact, while convenient for Parliament, created a great deal of ill will in the colonies. Many colonists believed that Parliament had no right to raise taxes when the colonies had no representation in Parliament, and they pointed to the fact that the King of England had long since surrendered any claim to raise taxes without the consent of the people's representatives in Parliament. A Parliament without a single American member, the colonists argued, could no more legally raise taxes on them than the King could on British citizens. Taxation without representation was, in the colonists' view, a violation of their rights as Englishmen.

The Sugar Act of 1764, the Stamp Act of 1765, and the Townshend Acts of 1767 had placed an increasing number of taxes and restrictions on the colonies, ostensibly designed to pay for the protection of the colonies, but colonial legislatures, including that of Virginia, saw these actions by Parliament as infringing on their traditional rights and prerogatives, particularly their sole right to raise and levy taxes within their boundaries.

Another issue the colonists had was even more intangible. The British colonies were restricted to a relatively narrow strip of land running from Canada in the north to Spanish-controlled Florida in the south, and between the Appalachian Mountains and the Atlantic Ocean. The colonies themselves had various border disputes with each other, but most importantly, if they were to expand (and the arrival of increasing numbers of colonists made this imperative), they could only do so to the west. However, in the wake of defeating the French, Britain had issued the Royal Proclamation of 1763, under which it provided assurances to Native Americans that it would limit colonial expansion beyond the Appalachian Mountains, guaranteeing that the tribal lands there would remain undisturbed. This was important to tribes such as the Miami, who had already seen the land they had previously lived on be taken by settlers. Further expansion would threaten their ancestral homelands.

Britain seemed content to keep the 13 colonies restricted mainly to the land east of the Appalachians, but many colonists saw this as an unreasonable restriction, imposed to specifically prevent the colonies from growing in size and becoming more powerful. In December 1773, the enmity between colonists and the British government led to the destruction of a shipment of tea in Boston Harbor.

Throughout this time, British officials tried to take advantage of their monopoly on trade with the natives by grossly overcharging or limiting supply in order to drive up prices, but several native tribes revolted, capturing six British forts in the region. In the Proclamation of 1763, trade goods were restored to previous levels and settlement was prohibited west of the Appalachians. The British assumed the French role of mediating tribal disputes and prevented a war between the Ottawa, Potawatomi, and Miami over western Ohio. Later, the Miami were able to act as mediators between the British and Kickapoo in 1765.

Tensions between Native Americans and the British colonists increased when settlers began violating the Proclamation of 1763 by moving into the Ohio Valley. The British could do little to stop this, however, as wealthy colonists had invested in the Ohio lands claimed by both Pennsylvania and Virginia colonies. Native tribes threatened to revolt, so British Indian agents met with the Iroquois at Fort Stanwix in New York in 1768 and convinced them to cede Ohio in order to protect their own homeland. The dozen other tribes who lived in the Ohio Valley, including the Miami, weren't consulted, but, most chose to concede rather than go to war with the Iroquois. In 1769, eastern groups of Miami abandoned western Ohio to the Shawnee and moved to Indiana, creating the two bands of the nation: the Indiana Miami and the Ohio Miami. In Lord Dunmore's War of 1774, the Miami remained neutral rather than face opposition from the Iroquois who were allied with the British.

The conflict between the natives and British was one of ideology more than race. For generations, native tribes had relied on open wilderness for their hunting grounds, providing them not only with food, but also clothes, household goods, and a myriad of other supplies made from various animal parts. The Europeans, and later Americans, on the other hand, sought to organize this wilderness into plots of land owned by families or the government for villages and farms. Natives grew hostile toward the settlers, whom they saw as invaders, restricting their hunting grounds by building forts, trading posts, farms, and towns, which in turn, restricted their way of life.

By the late 18th century, Miami material culture came to resemble that of the Europeans in many regards, while behaviors and beliefs remained tied to native culture. The Miami commonly used modern farm and construction tools and domestic items and clothing, which they obtained through trade, but their ceremonies and customs remained the same as they had for the last few centuries.

Under British control, the peaceful coexistence between Europeans and Indians began to fall apart. Strapped by debt, the colonial British government drastically reduced the budget of the Indian Agents, so individual speculators and traders were less regulated, and they entered native country in swarms. In 1768, the Six Nations Iroquois ceded land south of the Ohio River to the government, but speculators were not respectful of tribal boundaries and regularly entered lands uncontrolled by the Iroquois.

In July 1776, the Second Continental Congress issued the Declaration of Independence, a document explaining why the 13 colonies regarded themselves as states independent of Britain's governance. The document was revolutionary in every way, including its most famous passage: "We hold these truths to be self-evident, that all men are created equal, that they are endowed by their Creator with certain unalienable Rights, that among these are Life, Liberty and the pursuit of Happiness." At a time when many ordinary people in Europe were living in conditions indistinguishable from serfdom, the notion that all men were not only equal but had equal rights to liberty and happiness was seen as a serious threat to the established order, and Britain sent more troops to America in an attempt to crush the rebellion.

For all its lofty ideals, it was notable that, at least in the eyes of the Founding Fathers, "all men" did not include Native Americans. The same document that assured white settlers of their right to liberty and happiness also mentioned "the merciless Indian Savages whose known rule of warfare, is an undistinguished destruction of all ages, sexes and conditions."

Inevitably, during the war between Britain and the rebel colonies, many tribes felt compelled to take sides. Many chose to support Britain, believing this would provide better assurance of limiting the encroachment of settlers into Native American tribal lands. The resulting conflicts between the rebels and Native Americans were brutal in the extreme. American soldiers and militias treated Native Americans quite differently than British soldiers, and any who were captured could expect no mercy.

Even those Native American tribes choosing to support the patriots were not exempt from the violence. For example, Chief White Eyes of the Delaware tribe signed the Treaty of Fort Pitt in 1778. Under this treaty, the Delaware people and the patriots agreed to "perpetual peace and friendship," as well as the establishment of a Delaware state within the United States with representation in Congress. A few months later, however, a militia officer murdered Chief White Eyes, and later in the war, members of a colonial militia brutally killed dozens of unarmed Christian Delaware men, women, and children at the village of Gnadenhutten in Ohio. When the war ended, the promise of establishing a Delaware state with representation in Congress was conveniently and quietly forgotten.

The Miami people's reaction to the Revolutionary War was mixed. The Wea band remained largely neutral, while the Greater Miami generally supported the British. Some Piankeshaw villages supported the colonists, while others assisted the British. Fortunately for the Miami, the area in which they lived was not the scene of intense fighting, at least not until the arrival of a patriot force under the command of a French adventurer in October 1780.

Augustin Mottin de La Balme was a French cavalry officer who had fought against the British in Europe during the Seven Years' War before retiring in 1773 with the rank of fourier-major and spending his time writing about cavalry tactics. Like many cavalry officers of the era, La Balme was bold, impetuous, and filled with a strong (and possibly inflated) view of his own importance.

Augustin de La Balme

La Balme was inspired by reading the Declaration of Independence, so in 1777 the 44-year-old Frenchman traveled to the United States, assuming the patriots would welcome the services of an experienced senior cavalry officer. He was right, and he was quickly appointed as an inspector general of cavalry. He expected to be given overall command of all cavalry units in the Continental Army, but when he discovered that another European cavalry officer, Polish nobleman Casimir Pulaski, was to be given the role, he resigned in disgust.

In 1780, de La Balme traveled up the Ohio River to Kaskaskia in the Great Lakes region. There, he gathered a militia to march under the French flag in support of the patriot cause. Later, it would be claimed that de La Balme had done this because he was given secret orders for the mission by General George Washington, but it seems more likely that he acted on his own initiative.

Either way, de La Balme took his small force up the Maumee River headed for Fort Detroit, a large British outpost. His first objective was a trading post, located near the main Miami village at Kekionga. He took the trading post without opposition and camped there, waiting for reinforcements that never turned up. During the period in which de La Balme's force was close to Kekionga, many Miami warriors were absent, and the men of the militia also raided the village.

In a Miami village located on the Eel River not far from Kekionga, one warrior was so incensed by the attack that he asked the tribal council for permission to lead an attack on the de La Balme's forces. That warrior's name was Little Turtle.

Modern historians know relatively little about Little Turtle's early life. He was born around 1750 in a Miami village near Fort Wayne in Whitley County, Indiana, and survived a devastating smallpox epidemic in 1757, which killed large numbers of Miami. His mother was not a Miami, and most accounts suggest she may have been a Mahican, a descendant of survivors fleeing the destruction of that tribe by the Mohawk. His father was a chief of one of the Miami bands, but because he was not wholly Miami, Little Turtle was not eligible for the position despite the fact he distinguished himself in battle on several occasions in conflicts between the French and the British.

Even the name by which he is known to history is based on a misapprehension. His Miami name is usually given as Mishikinakwa, though there are several alternate spellings. This is because the Miami had no written language, so attempts to render Miami words into Latin characters were usually based on phonetic interpretations of spoken terms. Like many Miami, he was named after an animal, in this case a type of turtle found in rivers and lakes in the area in which the tribe lived. Where something approximating a signature was required, the Miami would simply append a sketch of the animal after which they were named. For this reason, Little Turtle's name is given in English as "Turtle," but it was believed (probably mistakenly) that his father was also known as Turtle, so the diminutive "Little" was added to distinguish the younger man.

By 1780, Little Turtle was about 30-years-old, strikingly tall, and a handsome man with a long face and full, high forehead only slightly marred by a large scar, the legacy of a slashing tomahawk wielded by a French soldier during a battle with the Miami in 1752. As a warrior, it is clear that Little Turtle was respected within the Miami, but there is little evidence that he was popular. He disdained the use of the alcohol, something many Miami had become enamored of, and he was prone to being sarcastic and cutting.

A contemporary depiction of Little Turtle

When he discovered that de La Balme had camped close to his village, he immediately requested permission to attack. This was given, and Little Turtle was appointed war chief. As Little Turtle prepared to attack, de La Balme was on the move. Leaving just 20 men to guard the captured trading post at Kekionga, the remainder of his force set off up the Eel River toward their final objective of Fort Detroit. On the evening of November 4, 1780, the force made camp on the banks of the Eel River. At dawn the following morning, Little Turtle and his Miami warriors attacked.

Details of precisely what happened are sketchy, but it seems that de La Balme's force attempted to fortify their camp to hold off the attack. They certainly held out for some time, though whether it was days, weeks, or even months varies in the accounts. The final outcome is not disputed: de La Balme's force was virtually annihilated, and though a few survivors did escape), de La Balme himself was killed. The battle, fought near present-day Columbia City, Indiana, became known simply as La Balme's Defeat.

A marker commemorating de La Balme's service for the patriots

This was a great victory for the Miami. La Balme's attack on Kekionga united the tribe against the fledgling United States, and La Balme's utter defeat was celebrated. At the same time, however, the battle made it clear that the Miami was an enemy of the Revolution as far as the colonists were concerned.

Little Turtle continued to serve as Miami war chief for the remainder of the war, leading a number of raids in support of the British against colonial settlements and militia units in present-day Kentucky. However, by early 1783, it was becoming clear that the British could not hope to win the war. They also faced rebellions in India and other places and simply did not have sufficient military might to fight simultaneous wars in several different theaters. As a result, the British government wanted to end the war in America as quickly as possible to focus on maintaining control over other parts of the empire.

Most Native American leaders who supported the British were not unduly concerned. After all, they had signed treaties with their British allies, providing binding agreements to maintain tribal lands. They were confident that any negotiations would uphold these treaties, but they were soon disabused of this idea.

Little Turtle's War

There was no legal, moral, or logical justification for Britain's cession of Native American land to the United States. The British had no rights to the land they handed over to the United States, and even some senior British government officials were horrified by those terms in the Treaty of Paris. Daniel Claus, a British government official in Canada, noted, It might have been easily reserved and inserted that those lands the Crown relinquished to all the Indn [sic]. Nations as their Right and property were out of its power to treat for, which would have saved the Honor of Government."

Ultimately, the British simply abandoned their obligations to former allies, and many Native Americans were coming to realize that "solemn and binding" treaties could be interpreted to mean whatever suited the white men. Making matters worse, the Miami found themselves living near people who believed them to be savages and blamed them for choosing to side with a tyrannical oppressor against a noble fight for liberty and equality. The treaties that had previously assured them of the right to their lands were simply abandoned, and they faced increasing numbers of settlers moving west. Conflict between the Miami and the United States seemed inevitable.

Nevertheless, the Treaty of Paris that concluded the Revolutionary War in 1783 established the borders of the new nation of the United States of America, giving it two frontier regions, the Northwest and Southwest Territories, in addition to the original thirteen colonies. The Northwest Territory, a huge swath of land between the Great Lakes, Mississippi River, and Ohio River, was home to numerous tribes, including the Miami Confederation. The Americans felt justified in treating the natives who had allied with the British as conquered enemies, refusing to recognize tribal sovereignty and allowing settlers to pour into the Ohio Valley. The weak American government based in Philadelphia had little control over westward expansion of settlers and did not enforce treaties with native chiefs. Thus, the Miami Confederacy stretched from Lake Erie to the lower Ohio River, barring settlement of the West.

Under Washington's leadership, the federal government attempted to negotiate with tribes in the area but made little progress, as the Miami and others rightly recognized that the only solution acceptable to the new federal government was to place settlers on Native American lands. Any negotiated settlement was bound to lead to the loss of their homelands, so the tribes had little incentive to talk. The situation was worsened by the enmity existing between the new administration and many Native American tribes, and the fact that many Americans regarded the Northwest Territory as a conquered land to which Native Americans no longer had any rights. It became rapidly clear that a negotiated settlement was not a viable option.

Various treaties were signed in the wake of the Revolutionary War, but few involved true negotiation. Native American representatives arrived to discuss the treaties, only to be presented with an ultimatum: give up land and peacefully accept settlers or face war with the United States. Some bowed to the demands. In the Treaty of Fort Stanwix, for example, some Iroquois tribes had agreed to give up much of their land in 1784. Pursuant to the Treaty of Fort McIntosh in 1785, the Delaware and Wyandot tribes made similar agreements.

In 1786, the federal government began negotiating the Treaty of Fort Finney in an attempt to persuade the Miami, Shawnee, and other smaller tribes to agree to move to an "Indian

Reservation" in the northern corner of Ohio. Although many bands were steadfastly opposed, the Shawnee leader signed the treaty. The Miami, however, remained united in their opposition. Not only did they refuse to sign the treaty, they also vowed to meet any further incursion into their lands with violent opposition if necessary.

This was a major problem for the American government, and not just for financial reasons. The American representatives at the treaty negotiations had been bluffing when they had threatened war if tribes didn't agree to move to reservation areas, and the truth was that the United States did not have a military force capable of mounting an expedition into hostile Native American lands. The Miami called this bluff.

In late 1786, representatives of several Northwestern tribes gathered to discuss their response to the American government. Some, including the Delaware and the Wyandot, were in favor of reaching a peaceful settlement, but the Miami and some Shawnee bands were completely opposed to that idea and pledged to fight to protect their lands. The Miami became the center of the opposition, and they quickly elected Little Turtle as war chief to direct action against the Americans.

President Washington was determined to prove that an egalitarian society governed by an elected administration was viable. This seems obvious now, but at the end of the 18th century, many people doubted that anything but a monarchy could lead a country effectively. To back away from expansion in the face of Native American opposition would make the new government look weak, both to its citizens and to other countries, including Britain, with which the United States hoped to create trading relationships. Washington was persuaded, albeit reluctantly, that the use of military force was the only way to make the Northwest Territory safe for settlement.

The commander of the national army at the time was General Josiah Harmar, a veteran of the Revolutionary War. When he took command in 1784, the entire military consisted of just 55 artillery officers at West Point and 25 more at Fort Pitt (present-day Pittsburgh). If required, these could be supplemented by additional troops from state militias, but these men were for the most part not sufficiently trained and poorly equipped.

Harmar

Somehow, Harmar would use the meager forces at his disposal to make the Northwest Territory safe for settlement. He was aware that he would be facing armed opposition from Native American people and wrote to Secretary of War Henry Knox, "The murders that have been committed lately upon the inhabitants passing up and down the Ohio, indicate great dissatisfaction prevailing amongst the Indians."

Under pressure from Harmar, the government finally agreed to the creation of a federal regiment, the First American Regiment, comprised of around 700 men. It was to be supplied and financed by the states of Pennsylvania, New Jersey, New York, and Connecticut.

A short time before Washington took the presidency, another Revolutionary War veteran, General Arthur St. Clair, was appointed governor of the Northwest Territory. St. Clair's mission was simple but challenging: he was directed to alleviate "all causes of controversy, so that peace and harmony may continue between the United States and the Indian tribes." In practice, he was to make the new territory safe for settlement by negotiating with Native Americans when possible and by other means if necessary.

St. Clair

St. Clair made several efforts to negotiate with the Northwestern tribes, but the Miami confederacy refused to consider giving up their lands. Ultimately, St. Clair agreed with Harmar that only force would compel the Miami to give up their lands. Thus, in 1790, the federal government decided to use military force to remove the Miami, and General Harmar was instructed to lead the national army, now expanded to include around 1,000 federal troops, supported by 1,500 militiamen from Kentucky, Pennsylvania, and Virginia. His orders from the government were to "extirpate, utterly, if possible, the Indian banditti."

In late 1790, Harmar set out from Fort Washington on the Ohio River (present-day Cincinnati). His main objectives were the Miami villages on the banks of the Maumee River, especially the main Miami village at Kekionga. Most Americans expected a quick victory against the intransigent Native American tribes, which was understandable given that the country had just cast off the most powerful nation in the world.

Little Turtle was aware well ahead of time of the impending arrival of the Americans. British and French fur traders in the area of the Maumee River had informed the Miami of the impending attack, in addition to providing them with guns and ammunition. Harmar did little to hide the advance of his force, probably hoping the threat alone would be sufficient to convince the Miami to capitulate. In fact, he insisted that his men march in tight formation, which was appropriate on the open battlefields of Europe, but the American forces were hopelessly unsuited to making progress through the rugged wilderness of the Northwest Territory. His men averaged less than 10 miles a day, and Miami scouts watched them continuously.

Harmar arrived at Kekionga on October 17, 1790 to find the village deserted and burning. He wrote a triumphant letter to President Washington on the same day, claiming that he had already won the war without firing a single shot. In reality, Little Turtle understood that meeting the Americans in an open battle would be a grave mistake, so he allowed them to enter Miami lands with the intention of orchestrating a guerrilla campaign of attrition.

On the very first night that Harmar's men were camped close to Kekionga, Miami warriors snuck into the camp unseen under cover of darkness and stole more than 100 horses, further hampering the mobility of Harmar's force. Harmar sent a part of his forces under the command of Colonel John Hardin of the Kentucky Militia to look for the Miami and the stolen horses. Hardin took 30 federal troops with him and around 150 militia, and as the force moved up the Eel River, they were ambushed by a band of Miami warriors led by Little Turtle. There were few survivors, and Harmar was visibly shocked when Hardin arrived back in the main camp with the tattered remnants of his force.

On October 20, Harmar decided to take his reduced force back to the safety of Fort Washington, but first he burned everything he could in Kekionga, including houses and food supplies that had been left behind. He hoped that this would at least deter the Miami from further aggression.

Though Harmar seemed content to flee, Hardin disagreed. Probably still horrified by his losses in the first engagement with Little Turtle's forces, Hardin proposed a ruse. The Miami would certainly be aware that the main force was retreating, and he reasoned they would most likely return to Kekionga after the American troops had left. Thus, a large force unexpectedly returned to the village, they might be able to surprise and engage the main force of Miami warriors.

Harmar agreed, and on the evening of October 21, Hardin took 60 soldiers and over 300 members of the Kentucky Militia back toward Kekionga. Little Turtle was waiting, again aware of the movements of the American forces. First, the Americans were ambushed as they crossed a ford on the Maumee River. Then, when Little Turtle feigned retreat, the Americans followed and stumbled into a second, even larger ambush. 50 federal soldiers and 68 militiamen died, and the remainder fled, with many of them wounded. The Miami called this the "Battle of the Pumpkin Fields" because the battlefield was left littered with the severed heads of so many fallen American soldiers.

When Hardin arrived at Harmar's camp, he claimed to have won a great victory, though it was readily apparent this was not so. Harmar continued back to Fort Washington, and when he arrived there on November , he, too, initially claimed to have won an important victory against the Miami.

Newspaper reporters interviewed survivors of his force and quickly deduced that this was not remotely the case. Many of those interviewed described Harmar as a coward (he had not personally been present during any fighting), an alcoholic, and an incompetent leader. The defeat at Kekionga became known among reporters as "Harmar's Defeat" and the "Battle of the Maumee."

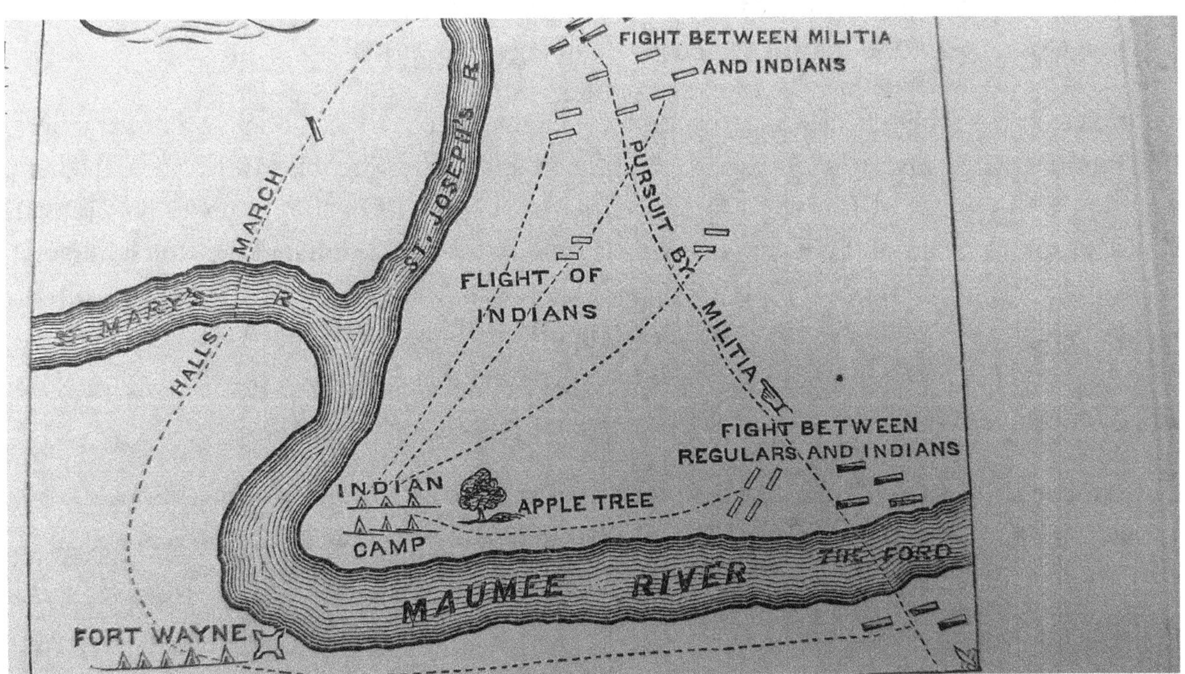

A map of Harmar's Defeat

As a direct result, Harmar was quickly dismissed as the head of the army and replaced by General St. Clair, still operating as the governor of the Northwest Territory. A quick victory against the Miami was essential for the federal government to allow settlement to continue, and to prevent other tribes from being persuaded that armed resistance had a chance of success. Harmar's defeat had seriously undermined confidence in the federal government, in particular its ability to protect its citizens in the Northwest Territory.

A resounding victory against the Miami was desperately needed, and St. Clair took his time gathering a powerful force. By October 1791, he had assembled a force of almost 2,000 men, comprised of 600 regular soldiers of the U.S> Army, 800 eight-month conscripts, and 600 militia, all supported by a strong contingent of artillery.

In late October, St. Clair led his army out of Fort Washington, accompanied by around 250 female camp followers, including wives, prostitutes, and workers. As before, his objective was the main Miami village of Kekionga.

St. Clair was confident that he would not face an open battle with the Miami. He expected the Native American warriors to continue their tactics of raids and ambushes as they had against Harmar's force. Once again, the Americans would find themselves outsmarted by Little Turtle.

Unknown to the Americans, Little Turtle had assembled a force of almost 1,000 warriors, mainly Miami but also including Shawnee and Delaware. By the time St. Clair had made camp on a hill near the headwaters of the Wabash River in the evening of November 3, desertion had reduced his force to only a little over 1,000 men and around 200 camp followers. Still confident he would not face a major attack, St. Clair failed to send out scouts to check the surrounding area, which proved to be a fatal mistake. During the night, Little Turtle moved his force closer, and the warriors hid in the forest, waiting for the first light of dawn.

As the troops began to rouse themselves on the morning of November 4, Little Turtle ordered the attack. First, the warriors attacked the militia, who broke and fled into the forest, leaving many of their weapons behind. The artillery was positioned on a bluff above the camp, and they wheeled into position in preparation to bombard the Native Americans. Little Turtle had foreseen this and had positioned a number of Miami sharpshooters in the woods nearby, who opened fire on the artillery crews and wrought such havoc that not a single shot was fired by any cannon.

Next, Little Turtle turned his attention to the main force of regular troops, already demoralized by the disappearance of militia units and the artillery's failure to provide covering fire. Both sides exchanged fire, and the Americans attempted several bayonet charges in an attempt to rout the Native American warriors. Each time, the Americans were allowed to advance before they were surrounded and attacked.

After three hours of fighting, St. Clair realized that he was facing not just a defeat but a catastrophe. He gathered his remaining officers and men and organized one last charge, intending to break through the Native American lines to escape. This was successful, but all artillery and supplies were abandoned, leaving the wounded and camp followers behind.

The remainder of St. Clair's force arrived at the safety of Fort Jefferson the following day and began to take stock. Of all the men St. Clair had led, only 24 escaped unharmed. Almost 80% of the officers were killed, while the casualty rate amongst the soldiers was close to 95%. No camp followers survived. In a single engagement, almost a quarter of the entire American military had become casualties. Over 800 Americans died that morning in the forests of the Northwest Territory, while Little Turtle is thought to have lost around 20 Miami warriors.

The sheer scale of the defeat was and remains unprecedented in American military history. More than three times as many American soldiers died at what became known as St. Clair's

Defeat than at the far more famous Battle of Little Bighorn about 80 years later. The casualty rate was the highest ever suffered by any American military unit.

President Washington was furious, and the government was stunned by the defeat. St. Clair was forced to resign, and a committee was formed to try to understand how this could have happened. This first-ever Congressional Special Committee found faults, not with St. Clair but with the initial creation and equipping of the army he led. St. Clair was formally pardoned from any responsibility for the defeat, but he was never reinstated as commander of the army

Plenty of Americans were openly critical of the federal government, and as far as it was concerned, this situation could not be allowed to stand. The Miami needed to be crushed, but the Americans would have to go back to the drawing board to determine how to accomplish it.

Naturally, the Miami and their supporters were overjoyed when they heard about the victories over Harmar and St. Clair, and Little Turtle became their most revered leader. Tribes such as the Ottawa and Wyandot, which had previously been reluctant to fight, were persuaded to join the confederacy led by the Miami after these victories. However, the harvest in the summer of 1791 had been poor, and most warriors were needed back in their villages to hunt for food for the winter, so the force assembled by Little Turtle for the battle against St. Clair was disbanded soon thereafter. There would be no attempt to follow up that victory with further attacks on forts or military outposts.

A Grand Tribal Council was convened in late 1791 to decide whether the war should be continued or if it was a good time to enter negotiations from a position of power. No final decision was reached, and it was agreed to defer a final decision until a meeting the following year. Meanwhile, the American government had sent emissaries to the Miami to discuss a possible end to the hostilities.

Negotiations began in early 1792 and included both the Shawnee and the Miami, but they achieved very little. The commissioners sent by the federal government pointed out that the land currently occupied by the Miami had been ceded to them by the British. The Miami explained that the lands did not belong to the British, and that the British had no rights to cede them to anyone. The Americans demanded that settlers be allowed into Miami territory, while the Miami demanded that settlers be confined to a line east of the Ohio River. Negotiations ended without any progress, a development that did not surprise either side.

The relationship between the federal government and Native American tribes in the Northwest Territory was certainly not improved by the murder of one of the American negotiators. Colonel John Hardin, the man who had led the Kentucky militia to disaster during the first attack on the Miami, was killed by the Shawnee in April 1792 after President Washington asked him to attempt negotiating with the tribe. It was clear to everyone involved that the differences between the United States and Native American tribes were so fundamental that they would not be solved through discussions.

Meanwhile, President Washington was dealing with a split within the government that reflected a wider difference of opinion among the American people. The disastrous campaigns of Harmar and St. Clair had focused attention on the government's attempt to expand to the west. Some people agreed and felt that the Native Americans resisting expansion should be crushed, but others felt that the whole notion of expanding into lands occupied by Native American tribes was misguided. One letter, published in the *Boston Gazette* in January 1792, asked, "Are we not already in possession of more lands than can be settled for a century at least?...What better right have we to march through the centre [sic] of their country, than Great-Britain [sic] would have to march a body of troops through the centre of the United States?" This view found a great deal of support in Congress, with some politicians seeing the attack on the Miami as a prelude to the creation of a professional standing army, and perhaps even as a ploy to mask the expansion of federal power. Others were concerned that relentless expansion made the nation seem avaricious, and its military's failure to accomplish this made the country look weak at home and abroad.

Ultimately, those who agreed with President Washington that expansion into Native American lands was the only way forward for the United States also theorized that the the the confederation of tribes led by the Miami might sweep east, attacking land presently controlled by the United States. It's now clear that was not something ever contemplated by the Miami, but at the time it seemed a real possibility, particularly given that the Americans had been mauled so recently. Furthermore, accepting the demands of tribes like the Miami would mean that the new nation would be limited to a strip of land on the East Coast, a notion that many of Washington's supporters found completely unacceptable. A letter published in the *Connecticut Gazette*, also in January 1792, noted that the battles against the Miami had been "[m]easures of necessity—The Indians had been invading our frontiers, and had killed many hundred innocent men, women and children."

In a sign of things to come, the government was split between the Democratic-Republicans, who believed that the federal government was using St. Clair's defeat to covertly increase its own power, and the Federalists, who supported President Washington and recognized the necessity of crushing the Miami. Understanding that the country's financial problems could be solved only by selling land in the Northwest Territory, the president harbored no doubt that there must be another expedition to confront Little Turtle and the Miami.

Supported by Secretary of War Henry Knox, Washington considered what needed to be done to create an army capable of fighting Little Turtle. The Militia Act of 1792 gave the federal government greater control over the militias, but it was also used to demonstrate that militias were not capable of effectively defending the citizens of the United States. The Act defined a total of almost 500,000 men who were theoretically capable of serving in these militias, but an investigation showed that less than 20% had the arms and equipment to serve effectively. Knox explained, "While it is acknowledged that mounted militia may be very proper for sudden enterprises, of short duration, it is conceived that militia are utterly unsuitable to carry on and terminate the war in which we are engaged, with honor and success."

Knox

Knox developed a proposal for a new professional army of over 5,000 men. This force, initially known as the Legion of the United States, would include units of cavalry, artillery, and both light and heavy infantry, combined into four sub-legions, each capable of fighting alone and each commanded by a Lieutenant Colonel. After a great deal of discussion in Congress, the proposal was accepted, and the man chosen to command the new force was Major General Anthony Wayne.

Wayne

Wayne was a veteran of the Revolutionary War, during which he earned the sobriquet "Mad Anthony" both for his boldness in battle and his irascible temper. Wayne played critical roles in several of the Revolution's most noteworthy campaigns, from the fateful Quebec invasion of 1775-1776 to the Yorktown campaign that ended the major fighting in 1781, with crucial actions at places like Valley Forge and Stony Point. He had been promoted to Major General by the time the war ended.

Knox reassured those opposed to the notion of a large standing army that this new force would only be required until "the United States shall be at peace with the Indian tribes." The creation of this army, combined with increased federal control over state militias embodied in the Militia Act of 1792, gave the federal government greatly increased power and direct control over the nation's military capability.

After traveling to Pittsburgh in June 1792, Wayne set about recruiting and organizing his forces, but he quickly had to deal with desertions and the jittery nerves of his own soldiers. He reported in August 1792, "Two nights since, upon a report that a large body of Indians were close in our front, I ordered the troops to form for action, and rode along the line to inspire them with confidence, and gave a charge to those in the redoubts, which I had recently thrown up in our front and right flank, to maintain their post at any expense of blood until I could gain the enemy's rear with the dragoons; but such is the defect of the human heart, that from excess of cowardice one third of the sentries deserted from their stations so as to leave the most accessible places unguarded."

Wayne decided that a long, rigorous course of training his new recruits would be necessary before he led them into battle, so he set up a training camp outside Pittsburgh which he called Legionville. In doing so, Wayne established the U.S. Military's first basic training facility.

There, his force stayed through the fall and winter, gaining the training and discipline necessary to become an effective fighting force. By the close of March 1793, he was able to report, "The progress that the troops have made both in manoeuvring and as marksmen astonished the savages on St. Patrick's day; and I am happy to inform you that the sons of that Saint were perfectly sober and orderly, being out of the reach of whiskey, which BANEFUL POISON is prohibited from entering this camp except as the component part of a ration, or a little for fatigue duty or on some extraordinary occasion."

A depiction of Wayne with the Legion

A modern picture of the site of Legionville

A marker at the site

At the same time, Wayne was aware that the prime function of the Legion was to defeat Native American tribes, so the training and organization of the new army reflected this. Rather than emphasizing drill and movement in large formations, troops were taught to fight in small units and to move quickly. Uniforms were designed differently due to the fact that during the battles fought by Harmar and St. Clair, Native American sharpshooters had targeted officers and successfully reduced the effectiveness of their units. With that in mind, the new uniforms made it deliberately difficult for an outsider to distinguish the officers from the men.

True to his reputation, discipline was harsh, and even minor infractions were severely punished. For example, any soldier found with a dirty uniform could be flogged.

In May 1793, Wayne moved his camp to Fort Washington, the present site of Cincinnati, where he received continual orders from the Secretary of War to avoid taking offensive operations against the natives while negotiations were going on. Naturally, Wayne chafed under the restraints, writing to the Secretary of War in October, "I will advance to-morrow with the force I have in order to take up a position in front of Fort Jefferson, so as to keep the enemy in check by exciting a jealousy and apprehension for the safety of their women and children, until some favorable circumstance or opportunity may present to strike with effect. I pray you not to permit present appearances to cause too much anxiety either in the mind of the President or yourself on account of this army. Knowing the critical situation of our infant nation, and feeling for the honor and reputation of the government (which I will support with my latest breath), you may rest assured that I will not commit the Legion unnecessarily. Unless more powerfully supported than I have reason to expect, I will content myself with taking a strong position in advance of Fort Jefferson, and by exerting every power endeavor to protect the frontier and secure the posts and the army during the winter, or until I am favored with your further orders."

Even as training continued at Fort Washington, Wayne realized that new forts would be required to provide the Legion with a safe refuge and a secure location for supplies. One of the most important of these was Fort Jefferson, located in present-day Darke County in western Ohio, deep within Miami territory. The fort had originally been built by St. Clair before his attack on the Miami, and it had come under attack on several occasions throughout 1792 and 1793. By November 1793, Wayne had moved a large force to the area and built a new fort, Fort Greenville, five miles to the north. The garrisons prepared to spend the winter in their new forts, located close to the site of St. Clair's defeat and within Miami territory.

In December 1793, Wayne sent eight infantry companies supported by artillery to the battleground on which St. Clair had been defeated. The area was a horrific sight, still scattered with the decaying remains of the unburied dead. Nevertheless, the Americans built yet another fort on the battlefield, which they named Fort Recovery. Wayne now had three forts deep in Miami territory from which he could threaten their heartlands in the spring.

A replica of Fort Recovery

Little Turtle, the Miami, and the other members of the confederation understood the threat the fortifications posed. From these, the Americans could strike at Kekionga and other Miami strongholds, so throughout that winter, the Native Americans mounted small-scale attacks on all three forts and supply trains.

By March 1794, the situation for Wayne was made more complex by Britain's intervention. Perhaps concerned at the United States' growing power and viewing the nation as a potential threat, the British Governor-in-chief of the Territory of Quebec, Lord Dorchester, announced that if the Legion were to "take possession of any part of the Indian Territory, this would be a direct violation of His Britannic Majesty's rights." This made little sense given that Britain had already ceded all rights to the land to the United States, but many people, including Little Turtle, assumed that a new war between Britain and the United States was imminent, and this seemed to be confirmed when the British built a new fort, Fort Miami, on the banks of the Maumee River, inside territory formally belonging to the United States. Bolstered by the presence of the British, and believing they would soon join the Miami in the fight against the United States, Little Turtle assembled a massive force of over 2,000 warriors from the Miami, Shawnee, and Delaware and prepared for an assault on the American forts in Miami territory.

In June 1894, Little Turtle led an attack on a supply train heading for Fort Greenville that had just left Fort Recovery. Although the Native Americans captured over 300 horses and killed 15 soldiers, the survivors were able to return to Fort Recovery and temporary safety. That night, the Native Americans mounted a full-scale attack on the fort, but the garrison put up a spirited defense and drove off their attackers. 23 soldiers were killed and 29 were wounded, but they held the fort. Somewhere between 50 and 100 Native American warriors died.

This was a serious setback for the Miami confederation. Fort Recovery was the smallest of the American forts in the area, and if they could not take it with such a large force, there seemed to be little hope the Native Americans could capture the larger forts. Little Turtle appealed to the British to provide him with soldiers and artillery, telling them that Wayne was a "black snake who never sleeps," but they declined. Disheartened, some tribes, most notably the Potawatomi, Ojibwa, and Ottawa, left the confederacy, seriously undermining its power.

Little Turtle was disheartened, believing that without the support of the British, the confederacy could not hope to win against Wayne and his forts. In July, he advocated making peace, but he was mocked as a coward by the more militant and aggressive war chief of the Shawnee, Blue Jacket (Weyapiersenwah). Blue Jacket was certain Wayne could be easily defeated, just as Harmar and St. Clair had. The confederation agreed, so Blue Jacket became war chief. Little Turtle agreed to continue to fight, but only as the leader of the Miami warriors.

In August 1794, Wayne led his force out of Fort Greenville to seek a final confrontation, and as before, he moved cautiously. The army built another fort, Fort Adams, in present-day Mercer County, Ohio, before moving on to the confluence of the Auglaize and Maumee Rivers, where yet another fort, Fort Defiance, was constructed. Finally, Fort Deposit was constructed, almost within sight of the British Fort Miami and close to Kekionga. Wayne sent the native tribes another overture for peace, one they spurned, and this led to one of the most consequential battles against Native Americans in history.

On August 20, the Legion left Fort Deposit and marched toward the Miami heartland. While building the various forts had provided Wayne with secure supply bases, the need to leave troops to guard each of them had reduced the size of his army to around 3,000 men. Neither he nor his army understood that they were marching toward an ambush set up by Blue Jacket. Over 1,000 warriors, including a large force of Miami under the command of Little Turtle, were lying in wait, concealed amongst fallen timbers close to the Maumee River.

In the morning, the lead elements of Wayne's army encountered the Native American ambush, but this time, the better trained and disciplined American troops did not break and run. Instead, they stood their ground and returned fire. Soon after, they were joined by the bulk of the Legion, and for just over an hour, the two sides fired at one another and made charges and countercharges.

Eventually, the Native American forces broke and fled, pursued by the Americans. Many fled to the nearby Fort Miami, assuming that the British would let them in, but the fort's commander,

Major William Campbell, closed the gates and refused them entry. He was justifiably concerned that if he aided the Native Americans, it might lead to fighting with American forces or even precipitate war between Britain and the United States.

As a result, the remnants of the Native American forces continued to flee to the north before making camp near Swan Creek. Disheartened by their defeat and their betrayal by the British, many refused to fight any more, and the army of the Miami confederacy practically disintegrated as the warriors trickled back to their homes.

On August 28, 1794, Wayne described the action in a letter written to the Secretary of War: "SIR,--It is with infinite pleasure that I now announce to you the brilliant success of the Federal Army under my command in a general action with the combined force of the hostile Indians and a considerable number of the volunteers & militia of Detroit (Canadians) on the 20th inst on the banks of the Miami in the Vicinity of the British post and garrison at the foot of the rapids....From every account the enemy amounted to 2000 combatants, and the troops actually engaged against them were short of 9oo. This horde of savages with their allies abandoned themselves to flight, and dispersed with terror and dismay leaving our victorious army in full & quiet possession of the field of battle which terminated under the influence of the guns of the British garrison, as you will perceive by the enclosed correspondence between Major Campbell, the commandant, & myself upon the occasion. The bravery & conduct of every officer belonging to the army from the Generals down to the Ensigns merit my highest approbation."

Casualties at what became known as the Battle of Fallen Timbers were relatively light on both sides - the Legion lost 30 killed and 100 wounded, while the Native American force lost 40 dead and an unknown number of wounded. However, the defeat marked the end of the Miami confederacy and the effective end of organized Native American resistance to the American settlement of Ohio. In December 1794, Wayne met with representatives from the confederacy to discuss peace terms. This led to the signature of the Treaty of Greenville in June 1795, under which the Miami and other tribes agreed to hand over the bulk of their lands in Ohio and territory in Indiana to the United States. The federal government also successfully pressured Britain to sign a treaty under which they would relinquish all their forts in the area. Little Turtle's War was over, and by the end of 1795, the Northwest Territory was firmly within the United States' grasp.

A painting of the treaty negotiations

An early 20th century commemorative stamp for Wayne and the Battle of Fallen Timbers

Little Turtle represented the Miami, but he was reluctant to sign the treaty and was the last member of the confederacy to do so. His wife died the following day and was buried by an honor guard from the Legion.

After the war, Little Turtle became an advocate for peace between Native Americans and settlers, and he even began to adopt an American way of life, including buying land from the federal government. He remained steadfastly opposed to the consumption of alcohol, and instead of being a war chief, he became the Miami peace chief and actively campaigned for smallpox inoculations for members of the tribe, among other things. In 1796, he was invited to Philadelphia to meet George Washington, who presented him with a ceremonial sword. He also later met President John Adams and President Thomas Jefferson, who encouraged Little Turtle and the Miami to adopt an American style of agriculture.

In 1809, Little Turtle broke with other Miami leaders over the signature of a new treaty, the Treaty of Fort Wayne, which ceded more Miami territory to the United States. As a result, he was no longer involved in Miami leadership and retired to live in a house built for him by the American government near Kekionga. During the War of 1812 between Britain and America, many Miami villages were destroyed, but Little Turtle's house was spared.

In July 1812, Little Turtle died at the home of his son-in-law, William Wells. He was 65-years-old and had suffered from gout and rheumatism for years. His funeral was held at Fort Wayne and included full military honors. He was buried in the Miami ancestral burial ground near Spy Run.

Little Turtle's War had a dramatic and lasting effect, not just on relations between the two sides, but on the nature of the new nation. Before Little Turtle's War, the United States was envisaged as being something radically different, not really a nation-state in the accepted sense, but a confederation in which real power was wielded by elected state legislatures and the federal administration provided only oversight and coordination between these states. The new country was not to have an army, but instead rely on state militias, with ordinary citizens taking up arms as required.

The catastrophic defeats of Harmar and St. Clair by Little Turtle forced a reappraisal of this view and the begrudging acceptance that if the United States wanted to take Native American lands in the Northwest Territory, a professional standing army under federal control was essential. Settlers wanted protection from Native Americans, and the federal government provided this, with the military becoming more powerful and more centralized in the process. Despite Henny Knox's reassurances, the Legion of the United States was not disbanded after the conclusion of the war. It was reduced in size and renamed the United States Army in 1796, but a professional standing army under federal control was here to stay.

Meanwhile, the white settlers' expansion into Native American lands continued after the end of the war. There were many confrontations between the U.S. Army and Native American forces, but nothing on the scale of St. Clair's defeat. The native resistance in the Northwest Territory would henceforth be led by the Shawnee, particularly Tecumseh and his brother, but their confederation would be defeated at the Battle of Tippecanoe in 1811. In the wake of that battle, the Northwest Territory was settled, and Native Americans were forced to live on reservations. In time, the new territory became the states of Ohio, Indiana, Illinois, Michigan, Wisconsin, and Minnesota.

Captives

In 1814, William Henry Harrison, the hero of Tippecanoe and the Governor of the Indiana Territory, recorded the change that alcohol had caused among the people he had once revered: "The Miami are merely a poor, drunken set diminishing every year, becoming too lazy to hunt," depending on their annuity from the U.S. government instead. In 1838, the Miami sold 177,000 acres of land in Indiana to the U.S. government, but, according to Young, "the proceeds were wasted for whiskey." Alarmingly, more than 500 Miami were killed between 1813 and 1830 in murders or accidents resulting from alcohol.

During the War of 1812 between the British and the U.S., the Miami remained largely neutral, but after Little Turtle's death, most of the Miami joined Tecumseh's alliance against the Americans, not only attacking U.S. forts and killing troops along with the British, but also raiding American settlements. One of Harrison's first actions as commander of American forces in the Northwest Territory was to attack the Miami villages on the Mississinewa River to prevent them from giving aid to Tecumseh. For the most part, native resistance ended with the death of Tecumseh at the Battle of the Thames in October 1813. The Second Treaty of Greenville in 1814 brought peace between the Americans and the tribes who had allied with them and the other tribes, including the Miami, who had fought with Tecumseh and the British.

Joseph "Peshewa" Richardville took over as chief after Little Turtle. The son of a noble French father and Miami maiden, Richardville had a unique ability to direct the affairs of the Miami while understanding the position of the settlers and their government. During his reign, there were no serious military troubles, so he was mainly a civil ruler and businessman. He ran a very prosperous trading business, and his mother conducted the tribe's portage business, transporting furs and other goods across the country on the Maumee and Wabash rivers. She held a monopoly on portage for many years and made large sums of money. She and her son received large tracts of land through treaties made with the U.S. government.

According to Young, Chief Joseph Richardville was thoughtful, patient, charitable, and intelligent. He spoke French and English as well as his native tongue. He tried his best to represent native interests, but pressure from the U.S. government was often too much. Amidst the conflict and warfare between white settlers and the Miami, hundreds were killed or captured by both sides.

Native tribes often took captives as a way to replace family members who had died, adopting them and treating them as their own. The remarkable stories of two such children remain significant. The first, Frances Slocum, was taken from her Quaker family home by three Delaware Indians in 1778 at the age of five. According to Arthur Lawrence Bodurtha's book *History of Miami County, Indiana,* Frances was hiding beneath the stairway when warriors ransacked the house. They dragged her from her hiding place and carried her away, along with a neighbor's child. Mrs. Slocum ran out of the brush and pled for her child's life, but the warrior threw five-year old Frances over his shoulder and hurried into the forest. The family reported the kidnapping to the military at nearby Wilkes-Barre Township, but the terrain and dangerous conditions made pursuit out of the question. For the next 30 years, Frances's brothers repeatedly attempted to find their sister, traveling all over the area, visiting native villages, and offering rewards for information, but their searches always came up empty.

According to Bodurtha, Frances's red hair made her a novelty almond the Indians, and they treated her with the utmost kindness. She was not abused or tortured, and she was eventually adopted by an older Delaware couple who had lost all of their children to war or disease. They gave her the name Weletawash, the name of their youngest child, whom they had recently buried. She was always treated kindly and was raised just like any other Delaware child would be.

At this time, the Delaware and Miami tribes lived together, and Frances eventually married a Miami chief called the Deaf Man. They moved to the new reservation west of the Mississippi River. She took the Miami name Maconaquah which means "young female bear." Bodurtha wrote that she was very skilled with a lariat and could run as fast as most of the men of her tribe. She had two sons, who both died in childhood, and two daughters, who lived to adulthood.

In 1834, an American trader was passing through and spent the night at the home of Deaf Man. He realized that Maconaquah was a white woman, though she dressed like a native and spoke the Miami tongue. Though she could remember little of her early life with her Quaker family, not even her Christian name, she told him her story, that she had lived happily as an Indian and never had a desire to return to her family. He wrote to the postmaster of Lancaster, Pennsylvania, hoping he could locate some member of her family. Two years later, the letter was passed along to Joseph Slocum, Frances's brother. Joseph, along with his brother Isaac and sister Mary, went to visit their long-lost sister. As they were strangers to her, she received them with indifference and declined to return home with her siblings, saying, "I have always lived with the Indians…I wish to live and die with them…this is my home. My husband and my boys are buried here and I cannot leave them. I have a house and large lands, two daughters…three grandchildren, and everything to make me comfortable, why should I go and be like a fish out of water?"

At the age of 13, William Wells was captured by a band of Miami near Louisville, Kentucky in 1784. He was adopted by Chief Porcupine, given the name Wild Carrot because of his red hair, and raised as one of his own, serving as an interpreter on numerous occasions. His brother found and visited Wells five years later, but he chose to remain with the Miami. He married Little Turtle's sister and fought alongside his brother-in-law against the U.S. Army under Harmar and St. Clair. He later negotiated for the return of several Indian hostages from U.S. custody. In 1794, he decided to return to his white family. He left the Miami village and joined the Americans under General Wayne as a spy. After the Treaty of Greenville, he rejoined his Miami wife and family and settled in an orchard at the confluence of the St. Mary's and St. Joseph rivers. He was later appointed Indian Agent at Fort Wayne, which he remained for several years, assisting Little Turtle in negotiations with the U.S. government. He and his Miami wives had four daughters and he was killed in a Potawatomi attack on Fort Dearborn in 1812.

Removal

Little by little, the Miami lands in Indiana were lost to treaties, debts, and taxes. Land treaties among various tribes between 1816 and 1820 ceded huge amounts of native lands to the U.S. government. The Miami and Wea relinquished almost 6 million acres but kept seven reserves in the northern part of Indiana. 19 Miami chiefs acquired separate sections of land for themselves.

Following the War of 1812, Americans assumed that the natives would be helpless without their British allies and would willingly cooperate with the requests of the U.S. government, but they were quickly proven wrong. In 1818, Indian Commissioner Benjamin Parke attempted to negotiate with the Miami, Weas, and Delaware, and from the very beginning things started badly, with all of the tribes arriving to the hearings two weeks late. Like most Americans, Parke had expected the natives to be ignorant savages, but Miami Chief Richardville was a well-bred gentleman of French descent and a shrewd businessman who was acquainted with the value of property, and he made things difficult for Parke. Richardville had never been the warrior that Little Turtle was, and he knew that well-defined and well-enforced property rights were a more effective way to protect the lands of the Miami than open warfare.

Unbeknownst to Parke, the chiefs had developed a plan long before their arrival. The Miami sub-chiefs and Mississinewa chiefs, who represented over eight percent of the Miami population, had agreed to walk out of the talks if the government refused to agree to their terms. As chief after chief rose from the bargaining table, Richardville remained behind until he was the last one left. He offered to convince the other chiefs to return to negotiations, but he insisted that it would require better terms. Parke agreed, and negotiations began anew. The chiefs left the table again when he refused to meet their demands, and Richardville again offered to bring them back. This cycle went on for weeks until Parke finally agreed to meet many of the Miami's demands.

At the conclusion of the proceedings, the U.S. government agreed to defend Miami lands from white settlers and gave huge land grants in fee simple to Richardville and his family and to the children of William Wells. The Miami would also be paid $15,000 annually in perpetuity.

Despite those dealings, in 1830, President Andrew Jackson signed the Indian Removal Act, which authorized the president to grant unsettled lands west of the Mississippi in exchange for Indian lands within existing state borders. This set in motion a chain of events that altered the existence of all native tribes on the continent. 10 years later, a treaty signed at the Forks of the Wabash ceded the last 177,000 acres of the Miami reserve to pay debts, and they agreed to be removed to Indian Territory in Kansas within five years. Chief Meshingomesia's band was allowed to stay in Wabash County, Indiana because he owned the land in fee simple, and this would lead to a permanent split in the Miami nation. Henceforward, the Ohio Miami and the Indiana Miami would exist as two separate tribes.

Richardville died in 1841, and his son-in-law Francis La Fontaine became the chief afterward, so it was up to him to guide the 600 members of his tribe in compliance with the Treaty of 1840. Several of his people refused to leave, and the U.S. government stepped in to remove them by force. Some attempted to escape into the forest and had to be tracked down. Some fled and were arrested upon their return to their former homes and then taken to Kansas as prisoners. Most were marched at gunpoint to canal boats to travel down the Erie Canal system to the Ohio River, then took steamboats down the Ohio and Mississippi Rivers to Missouri. They traveled on horseback and in wagons the remainder of the journey to a reservation in Kansas. La Fontaine moved to the reservation, but he was never satisfied with life there and chose to return to Indiana. During the trip back to Indiana, he became ill and died at Lafayette, Indiana on April 13, 1847 at the age of 37. Some Miami eventually returned to their homeland, living as vagrants, while a few village chiefs who agreed to the government's terms were rewarded by being allowed to retain their lands.

Unlike their homelands, this area consisted mostly of tall grass prairie. The Miami rebuilt their homes, planted corn, and continued to hunt deer and bison as they always had, but the reservation was a poor substitute for the lush, abundant wilderness of their homelands. Almost a third of the Miami died during the first year in Kansas, and Mrs. Mary Batiste Peoria, the wife of the American agent there, wrote that she saw strong men weeping with homesickness. Some left the reservation to return home without even shoes on their feet or a crust of bread to eat. In 1848, historian John B. Dillon wrote, "At the present day, a few small, mixed and miserable bands constitute the remnant of the once powerful Miami nation…the last fragments of one of the most powerful aboriginal nations of North America are passing away from the earth forever."

Within a decade, the U.S. government was eager to open Kansas for settlement and to facilitate construction of a transcontinental railroad, so they sought to purchase the land the Native Americans had recently been resettled on. In June 1854, the Miami and Peoria tribes ceded more than 500,000 acres in exchange for 200 acre individual allotments, but no offer of citizenship was made in return. In 1862, Kansas became a state, and its legislature asked the federal government to remove the Native Americans. The Civil War put this request on hold, but in an omnibus treaty in 1867, the Miami, Peoria, Wea, Ottawa, Seneca, Wyandot, Delaware, and Shawnee ceded their last Kansas lands and agreed to be removed to Oklahoma. They purchased 6,000 acres in the northwest corner of the state in present-day Ottawa County, and with that, the various tribes, some of whom were bitter enemies, were all resettled together.

By this time, there were only about 100 remaining adults in the western Miami group. In the 1880s, the Miami reserve area was broken up into family allotments and deeded to individual tribal members. On these lands, families used annuity funds to build homes and barns and purchase equipment to establish farms on their lands. A few such homes still remain in the Miami reservation area.

In 1897, the Assistant U.S. Attorney General terminated the tribal status of the Indiana Miami, giving no explanation for this action, but the Oklahoma Miami never lost federal recognition. This means that the Oklahoma Miami has its own government, laws, police, and services, and they are also U.S. citizens.

In 1936, the Oklahoma Indian Welfare Act led to the Miami being officially recognized as a sovereign nation. They soon established their first Tribal Constitution, and since then they have been governed by an elected leadership called the Tribal Business Committee, consisting of a Chief, Second Chief, Secretary-Treasurer, and two Councilpersons. The Committee works to retain tribal language, customs, and heritage and to ensure that tribal lands are used in culturally appropriate ways and that the new generations are educated appropriately.

The Indiana Miami, on the other hand, are not federally recognized, so they do not enjoy their own government or reservation lands, but they still have traditional leadership and tribal meetings. They have challenged their non-recognized status for over a century and always refer to themselves as a tribe or nation. They are mainly a rural people.

By the 1950s, only a handful of Miami owned a few acres in Indiana, and many expected the complete disappearance of the Miami tribe due to loss of population or total assimilation into American culture. Tribal craft activity, including clothing, beadwork, and metalwork was almost nonexistent, the spoken language was going extinct, most folklore and subsistence activities were gone, and most tribe members were married to non-Indians. However, in the 1960s, the Miami began to revitalize themselves as a tribe, partly because of national trends in Native American awareness and the help of the Indian Claims Commission. By the early 1990s, they had emerged as a full-fledged tribal organization, able to provide support and services to its people even without federal recognition. In Peru, Indiana, seat of Miami County, visitors can find tribal headquarters, an extensive tribal archive, a cultural center and small museum. The tribe owns 35 acres of land with a longhouse for traditional ceremonies.

Today, northeast Oklahoma is the seat of government for the sovereign nation of the Miami tribe, which maintains a 1,400-acre land base and many tribal businesses in and around the town of Miami, Oklahoma. There are now more than 5,000 Miami in Oklahoma and 2,500 in Indiana. The Myaamia Center at the Miami University of Ohio works to strengthen the Miami Nation through revitalization of their distinct customs, language, and culture through research, awareness, and preservation.

Needless to say, the Miami's history, for better and worse, remains an important part of the nation's experiences. This ancient group has relied on a collective memory to provide continuity in the face of drastic changes, and the history ultimately helped them to survive as a people. As active shapers of their own destiny, the modern Miami people cling to their proud heritage and culture, which has remained strong despite centuries of conflicts with other tribes, Europeans, and Americans, and they have managed to weather the loss of their homelands, age-old customs, and ways of life. Despite everything, from the lush river valley woodlands of Indiana to the rolling prairies of Oklahoma, the Miami have survived and persevered.

Online Resources

Other books about Native American history by Charles River Editors

Other books about the Miami on Amazon

Further Reading

Bodurtha, Arthur Lawrence. *History of Miami County, Indiana.* <http://genealogytrails.com/ind/miami/frances-slocum.html>

Carr, Karen. "Algonquin History: Early Native Americans." <https://quatr.us/nativeamerican/algonquin-history-native-americans.htm>

"Medicine Society." Encyclopedia Britannica. 02 July 2017. <https://www.britannica.com/topic/medicine-society>

"Native Languages of the Americas: Miami Legends, Myths and Stories." <http://www.native-languages.org/miami-legends.htm>

Rafert, Stewart. *The Miami Indians of Indiana.* Indiana Historical Society. 1996.

Shepherd, Joshua. "William Wells." <https://warfarehistorynetwork.com/2019/01/15/william-wells/>

Sultzman, Lee. "Miami History." First Nations. 1999. <http://www.tolatsga.org/Compacts.html>

The Miami Tribe of Oklahoma. "History." Kiiloona Myaamiaki. <https://www.miaminiation.com/node/11>

Young, Calvin. *Little Turtle: The Great Chief of the Miami Indian Nation.* 1917.

Free Books by Charles River Editors

We have brand new titles available for free most days of the week. To see which of our titles are currently free, click on this link.

Discounted Books by Charles River Editors

We have titles at a discount price of just 99 cents everyday. To see which of our titles are currently 99 cents, click on this link.